EARTH'S RESOURCES

OIL AND GAS

NEIL MORRIS

W
FRANKLIN WATTS
LONDON•SYDNEY

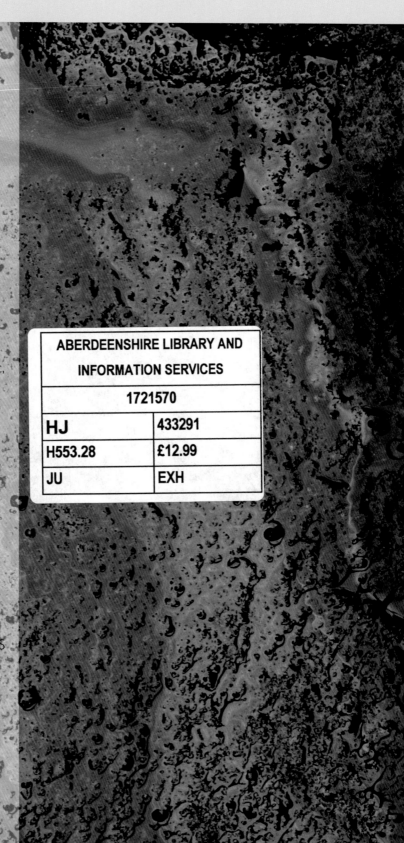

 An Appleseed Editions book

First published in 2005 by Franklin Watts
96 Leonard Street, London, EC2A 4XD

Franklin Watts Australia
Level 17/207 Kent Street, Sydney, NSW 2000

© 2005 Appleseed Editions

Created by Appleseed Editions Ltd,
Well House, Friars Hill, Guestling, East Sussex,
TN35 4ET

Designed by Guy Callaby

ISBN 0 7496 5992 0

A CIP catalogue for this book is available from the
British Library.

Photographs by Corbis (HEINZ-PETER BADER /
Reuters, Bettmann, Peter Blakely / CORBIS SABA,
Fabian Cevallos / CORBIS SYGMA, Marco
Cristofori, Derek Croucher, Barbara Davidson /
Dallas Morning News, J. A. Giordano/ CORBIS
SABA, Lowell Georgia, Chinch Gryniewicz;
Ecoscene, Hulton-Deutsch Collection, Layne
Kennedy, Matthias Kulka, Jacques Langevin/ CORBIS
SYGMA, Larry Lee Photography, Lester Lefkowitz,
Lucidio Studio Inc., José F. Poblete, Roger
Ressmeyer, Reuters, MAIMAN RICK / CORBIS
SYGMA, ROSHANAK.B / CORBIS SYGMA,
Charles E. Rotkin, Royalty-Free, Michael St. Maur
Sheil, Paul A. Souders, Steve Starr, Vince Streano,
David Turnley, Doug Wilson, Douglas P. Wilson;
Frank Lane Picture Agency, John Zoiner), Getty
Images (Lester Lefkowitz, Robert Stahl)

Printed in Thailand

CONTENTS

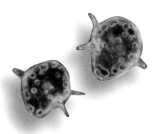

INTRODUCTION

Oil is one of the world's most valuable resources. It is used both as a source of energy and as a raw material for making many other things. It is also called petroleum, which comes from the Latin words for 'rock oil'. People may have given this name to the substance in ancient times because they found small amounts of it seeping from rocks in the ground.

Today we get huge quantities of oil from deep beneath the Earth's surface. This is also where we look for natural gas, which is often found on top of oil deposits. Both oil and gas are made up of hydrocarbons, which means that they contain the gas hydrogen and the element carbon. The deposits that we use today were formed many millions of years ago, but they will not last forever.

When people strike oil, they strike it rich. But most oil fields are owned and run by huge companies rather than individuals.

Black gold

Oil is sometimes called 'black gold', because it is so valuable. Although oil is no longer stored in wooden containers as it sometimes was years ago, it is still measured and sold in quantities called barrels. One barrel of oil is equal to about 159 litres, and 8 barrels of oil weigh about a tonne. Amazingly, we produce and use more than 75 million barrels of oil around the world every day. The price that suppliers charge for oil is very important, because the world is so dependent on its oil. When oil prices go up, the cost of many other things goes up too.

These pipelines carry natural gas from wells in northern Russia.

Natural gas

The gas that we find underground occurs naturally. It is made up mainly of a hydrocarbon gas called methane. We call it natural gas to distinguish it from an earlier form of fuel, also called gas, that was made by heating coal. This manufactured coal gas was sometimes called 'town gas', because it was piped to people's homes. Today most of the gas used as fuel for heating homes and cooking is natural gas. We produce more than 7 million cubic metres of natural gas every day, which would fill more than 44 million oil barrels with gas.

These barrels of oil are ready to be delivered to customers. The red-and-yellow drums are marked with the symbol of one of the world's largest oil companies, Shell.

WHERE IN THE WORLD?

Oil and gas are found on all of the world's continents and under the seabed of all of the world's oceans. This means that oil and gas industries operate worldwide, except on the frozen continent of Antarctica, where international agreements prevent mining or drilling.

The world's biggest producer of oil is Saudi Arabia; experts believe that the surrounding Middle East region holds about two-thirds of the world's oil reserves. The next-largest producer is the United States, which uses far more oil and gas than any other nation and therefore has to import a large amount. Next comes Russia, which also produces more natural gas than any other country. The US and Canada are second and third among natural gas producers.

An oil-well pump, called a 'nodding donkey', working at Lake Maracaibo in Venezuela. This South American country has the most known oil reserves outside the Middle East.

Arabian oil

The discovery of oil in the Arabian Desert in 1936 brought great wealth to the countries of the region. The world's largest oil field lies in a desert area of the region's biggest country, Saudi Arabia. The Ghawar oil field began production in 1951. More than 50 years later, it was still producing more than four million barrels a day – about half the Saudi total. Saudi Arabia uses less than a fifth of the oil it produces. Much smaller neighbouring countries, such as the United Arab Emirates, Qatar and Kuwait, are also large producers of oil.

An oil well in the Saudi Arabian desert. Oil is shipped all over the world from Saudi ports on the Persian Gulf.

The town of Novyy Urengoy lies just south of the Arctic Circle in northern Russia, more than 2,000 kilometres from the capital Moscow. The town began as a workers' settlement in 1973 and now has a population of about 90,000.

Arctic gas

Russia's most productive gas fields are in the Siberian north of the country, near or even above the Arctic Circle. This is a very cold region, especially during the long, hard winters, and small settlements have grown into towns to house workers and their families. Russia produces more gas than it uses, and long pipelines have been built west to Europe and east to Asia. A new gas pipeline is currently being built from Siberia to China and South Korea.

HOW OIL AND GAS FORMED

Millions of years ago, the world's oceans were full of tiny animals and plants. When these microscopic organisms died, their remains sank to the seabed. There they were covered by mud and sand, which formed layers as more dead remains sank down on top.

Over very long periods of time, the rotting remains were squashed and heated by the weight of the layers above. These actions turned the remains into oil, which also gave off bubbles of natural gas. During this process, the heat and pressure changed the layers of mud and sand, or sediments, into sandstone and other kinds of rocks. The oil and gas flowed into holes in the rocks, but layers of non-porous, or completely solid, rocks above trapped the oil and gas.

These tiny organisms, called plankton, drift near the surface of oceans. The dead remains of such organisms formed oil and gas.

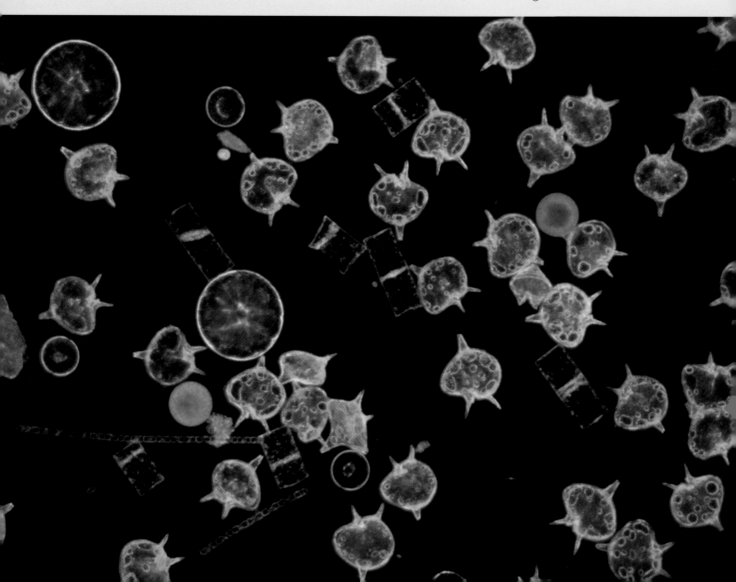

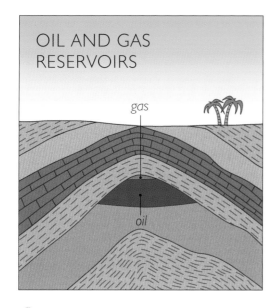

OIL AND GAS
RESERVOIRS

gas

oil

After forming – at a temperature between 100° and 200° centigrade – oil and gas move up through porous rocks until they are trapped in pockets or reservoirs.

The black pitch of Pitch Lake, Trinidad, is thick and gooey.

Fossil fuels

Because they come from the fossilized remains of prehistoric plants and animals, oil and gas are called fossil fuels. The world's other fossil fuel is coal. While the fossil fuels were forming, the surface of Earth was changing. Great movements in the earth's crust meant that many areas of seabed were raised above the ocean surface and became land areas. Some of these areas are now desert, such as the oil-rich regions of the Middle East. Others remain offshore, such as the oil and gas fields of the North Sea.

Pitch Lake

In some places oil seeps up through cracks in rocks to form natural deposits on the surface. The deposits are usually of a thick, heavy substance that we call asphalt (or sometimes bitumen or pitch). They are often found in pits or lakes, and one of the most famous examples is Pitch Lake, on the Caribbean island of Trinidad. It was probably known and perhaps used by local Arawak and Carib people for centuries before being found by British explorer Sir Walter Raleigh in 1595. We know that many ancient peoples used pitch to waterproof their boats.

EXPLORATION

Finding oil used to be mostly a matter of luck, but today's geologists and oil surveyors use scientific methods that make success more likely. First, they can identify promising sites by looking at satellite images and aerial photographs. A dome-shaped hill, for example, might suggest that oil and gas are trapped below.

Once they have identified a potential region, the surveyors use a variety of instruments to check it further. A gravimeter, or gravity meter, can be used to measure differences in the pull of gravity, providing information on the kinds of rocks below the surface. In a similar way, a magnetometer measures changes in Earth's magnetic field, showing where there are faults in sedimentary rocks. Many tests are carried out on land, while others are made at sea.

Surveyors search for likely places to drill for oil and gas. In the frozen Arctic, they have to check the movement of ice.

Checking vibrations

Scientists use seismographs to measure and study earthquakes, but these sensitive instruments can also be used to find oil. Surveyors sometimes set off small test explosions so that they can test shock waves as they bounce off different layers of rock. A careful check of the results gives an idea of where pockets of oil might be located. To avoid using explosives, vibrations can also be set off by thumping the ground hard with a large, metal plate.

Special 'thumper trucks' are driven to promising locations and used to cause vibrations that can be measured.

Wildcats and dry holes

When a good potential site has been found, the decision may be made to drill a test well, which oil and gas workers call a 'wildcat'. Nine times out of 10, this turns out to be a 'dry hole' that contains no oil or gas, or it may have a very small amount that is not worth the expense and trouble of setting up a production rig. On the rare occasions that good quantities of oil and gas are found, the site is prepared for the construction of the steel framework that will hold the drilling equipment. This is called a derrick. If the site is in a remote part of the world, roads may have to be built to allow equipment to be brought in.

This oil derrick has been set up in Alaska.

DRILLING

Oil and gas are extracted by drilling down through rocks to reach the pockets where they are located. The drilling is done by a sharp-toothed bit that is attached to the end of a series of linked steel pipes called a drill string. The spinning bit cuts a hole through the rocks, and as the drill string is lowered into the ground, more sections of pipe are added to it.

Mud is pumped down the pipes, flowing back up the hole and carrying material to the surface. This drilling mud helps to cool and clean the bit, which has to be hauled back up to the surface when it needs changing. In most cases the drill string is many thousands of feet long. Changing and adding sections is hard, dangerous work. It is done by oil-rig workers known as roughnecks.

Drill ships are used in deep water. The drill is operated from a control room, which uses computers to keep the ship and drill in exactly the right place.

Turntables and turbodrills

Roughnecks work at the platform turntable, which is clamped on to the drill string. The turntable is driven by a diesel engine and turns the whole string and the bit. It has to be stopped when new lengths of pipe are added. Later, more steel pipes are lowered into the drilled hole to act as a casing. More modern high-speed turbodrills use mud to power a turbine that spins inside the drill string near the bit. Turbodrills are also used for directional drilling, in which the well hole can be cut at an angle or in a curve instead of straight down.

Workers add a length of pipe to the drill string. A team of roughnecks is supervised by a driller.

Offshore rigs

In shallow water near the coast, so-called jack-up or fixed-leg rigs stand on the seabed. In deeper water, floating rigs have huge buoyancy tanks to keep them afloat and stable. They have a large, flat production platform for the derrick and other equipment. The platform also houses living quarters for all the workers, as well as a landing pad for the helicopters that carry workers to and from the shore. The rig may also have storage tanks around its legs, or it may be linked to onshore tanks by pipelines laid on the seabed.

An offshore rig in the North Sea, where oil and gas have been produced for Britain, Norway and other European countries since the 1960s.

FROM RIG TO REFINERY

When a drill string has almost reached the depth at which the drilling team expects to reach oil or gas, the well is prepared for production. The bit is hauled up, tubing is lowered into the well hole, and a small explosive device is used to blast away the rock above the oil pocket.

Oil then gushes up the tubing and is controlled by a set of valves on the rig platform. If this process is not followed carefully, or if oil is struck earlier than expected when drilling, there may be a blow-out. This can be dangerous and is wasteful. Once the flow of crude oil has been properly controlled, it is channelled through pipes to a storage tank. It is then ready to be delivered to a refinery.

This worker is operating a complicated set of valves above an oil well.

Trans-Alaska pipeline

Oil was discovered on the north coast of Alaska in 1968. Nine years later, a 1,300-kilometre pipeline had been built between Prudhoe Bay, on the Arctic Ocean, and the port of Valdez on Alaska's southern, Pacific coast. More than a million barrels of crude oil are pumped along the 1.2-metre-wide pipeline every day, taking nine days to make the journey from coast to coast. At Valdez, the oil is first stored in 18 vast tanks before being transferred to ships docked at one of the port's four berths. The tankers then carry the oil to ports on the west coast of the US and elsewhere.

The Trans-Alaska pipeline crosses three mountain ranges and more than 800 rivers and streams. In parts, it is raised 3 metres above the ground so that herds of caribou and other animals can pass underneath.

Supertankers

Some of today's oil tankers are enormous vessels called 'very large crude carriers' (VLCCs). Those that can carry more than 300,000 tonnes of cargo are called ULCCs – 'ultra large crude carriers'. Such huge supertankers need very large ports to load and unload their cargo, and many ports are offshore terminals served by underwater oil pipelines. The biggest ULCC of all is the *Jahre Viking*, which is 458 metres long, 69 metres wide, and can carry more than four million barrels of oil.

Supertankers take more than 8 kilometres to stop. Docking is not easy!

REFINING CRUDE OIL

Crude oil is not used in the same form that comes out of the ground, but is changed into many different kinds of oils and gases at a refinery. These various substances, such as kerosene and petrol, are all mixtures of hydrocarbons.

They are each made up of different combinations of hydrogen and carbon. At the refinery, the crude oil is heated by a furnace to 400° centigrade before passing into a tall steel column called a fractionating tower. The tower is hottest at the bottom and coolest at the top, and the different kinds of oils and gases boil (and turn into gas) and condense (and turn back into a liquid) at different temperatures. This is not the end of the process at the refinery, which has many more pipes, tanks and processes. Heat, pressure and chemicals are also used to change one combination of hydrocarbons into another.

This oil refinery in Canada has several steel fractionating towers. Refineries operate day and night, and the processes are shut down only occasionally for maintenance.

Light and heavy fractions

The different groups of oils and gases are called fractions. In the fractionating tower (given this name because it divides crude oil into fractions), groups of hydrocarbons with high boiling points condense first, at the bottom of the tower. Those with lower boiling points condense higher up the tower, where they collect on trays and flow out of the tower through individual pipes. Some groups, such as butane and propane, have such low boiling points that they remain as gases and exit at the top of the tower.

From petroleum to petrol

Petrol condenses out of petroleum at a low temperature of between 30° centigrade and 80° centigrade. This is the most important product of the refining process, because it is used as the main fuel for cars. More than a third of the world's petroleum (crude oil) is refined into petrol. We use so much petrol that other processes are used in the refinery to change heavier fractions into lighter ones such as petrol.

A worker climbs to the top of a fractionating tower to check it from the outside.

Tanker trucks carry petrol and other refined oils to petrol stations, chemical factories and other locations.

STARTING AN INDUSTRY

Ancient peoples used pitch to waterproof baskets and boats, but the real history of the use of oil began in the 19th century. Small oil springs were found in England and the US, and people began digging pits to gather the oil.

Then, in 1859, a retired railway conductor named Edwin Drake took charge of some oil pits near Titusville, Pennsylvania, and tried out a new idea. He drilled a well and lined it with an iron pipe. When the steam-driven drill reached a depth of about 29 metres, it struck oil. Soon Drake was filling old wooden whisky barrels with the 'black gold', which he raised using a hand-operated pump. As the news spread, people hoping to strike oil rushed to Pennsylvania, where the first oil pipeline flowed in 1865. People also started drilling in other parts of the world where traces of surface oil had been found.

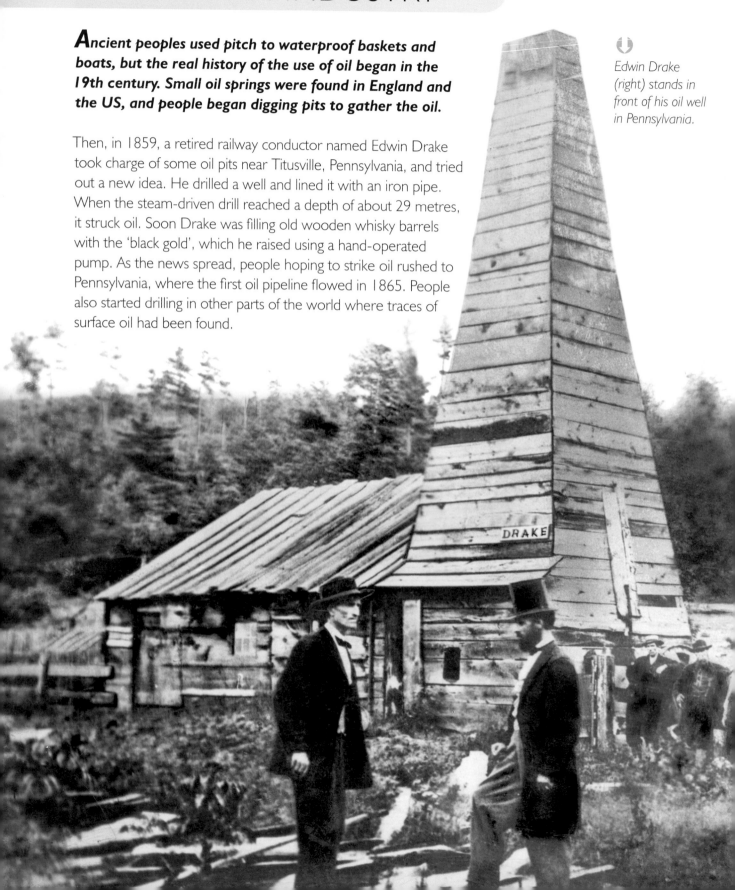

Edwin Drake (right) stands in front of his oil well in Pennsylvania.

Oil in the Middle East

In 1890 a French geologist discovered that there was oil beneath the desert of Persia (present-day Iran). Eighteen years later, oil was flowing from a Persian well and, by 1913, more than 2,000 barrels of crude oil were being delivered daily to Persia's first refinery. In 1951 the Iranian oil industry came under government control, and today it is the fifth-biggest producer of oil in the world (and the 10th-largest producer of gas). Oil was first discovered on the other side of the Persian Gulf, in Saudi Arabia, in 1936.

A Persian oil derrick photographed in 1909, exactly 50 years after Drake's first Pennsylvanian well.

A conference of energy ministers at OPEC headquarters in Vienna, Austria.

OPEC

In 1960 representatives of five countries – Iran, Iraq, Kuwait, Saudi Arabia and Venezuela – formed the Organization of the Petroleum Exporting Countries (OPEC). The idea of the organization was to coordinate the different nations' interests in their dealings with large oil companies in other countries. They particularly wanted to agree on, and control, the price of a barrel of oil. OPEC is still an important, powerful organization today. It has six more members – Algeria, Indonesia, Libya, Nigeria, Qatar, and the United Arab Emirates – and together the OPEC countries produce 40 per cent of the world's oil.

GAS HISTORY

The ancient Chinese may have been the first people to use natural gas. We know that they drilled for salt more than 2,000 years ago, and historians believe that they found gas at the same time.

They probably transported the gas through bamboo pipes and burned it to heat pans full of salty water, so that it boiled and they could recover the salt. Before 600 AD, people were worshipping at temples with 'eternal fires' near the Caspian Sea (in modern Azerbaijan). Many thought that the fires were the result of a divine miracle, and merchants and others travelled long distances to visit them. In fact, the temple fires were produced by lighting gas that sprang naturally from cracks in the ground nearby.

The Ateshgyakh Fire-Worshippers' Temple, at Baku in Azerbaijan, is lit by natural gas that escapes through underground cracks. Many Zoroastrians, who worshipped fire, believed that the flames had divine power.

Coal gas

Gas was first made by heating coal in the early 17th century. Later, in 1792, a British engineer named William Murdock found a way to light his home with gas he made from coal. It was not long before Murdock's invention was being used to light factories and, in 1807, the first gaslights were used on London streets. This seemed an amazing advancement to ordinary people and gas lighting was very popular. By 1819, there were more than 450 kilometres of gas pipes in the English capital.

A lamplighter adjusts a London gaslight in 1935. By then much of the city was lit by electricity.

Lighting Fredonia

In 1821 a gunsmith named William Hart heard that people had seen mysterious bubbles rising in a creek near Fredonia, New York. That same year, Hart dug a well 8 metres deep and discovered natural gas. He also worked out a way to pipe the gas through hollowed-out logs. This allowed him to use the gas to light nearby shops, mills and inns. Others built much longer wooden and iron pipelines in the 1870s and, by 1900, natural gas had been discovered in 17 US states. Huge gas reserves were found in the southern US in the early 20th century.

As more and more gas and oil deposits were discovered, drilling equipment improved.

STORING AND DELIVERING GAS

Natural gas is first piped from the original well to a processing plant. There impurities and other gases, such as butane and propane, are removed. The natural gas, which is mainly methane, is then fed under pressure into underground pipelines, where it travels along at about 15 miles an hour.

In the 1900s manufactured gas was often stored in towns and cities in large metal gasholders, or gasometers, but today most natural gas is stored underground. Old salt mines and natural salt caverns are often used. Storage is important because the demand for gas changes throughout the year and is particularly high in winter, when much more gas is needed for heating homes.

A group of gasometers was built around the gasworks in Vienna, Austria, in 1899. They stored town gas, but now that Austria uses natural gas, the gasometers have been turned into shopping centres and apartment complexes.

Gas in the home

Since natural gas has no smell, gas companies add a chemical so that any leaks are easily noticed. From transmission pipelines and storage units, natural gas moves though towns and cities along large underground pipes called gas mains. Smaller pipes, called service lines, branch off from the mains and lead to individual homes and other buildings. Inside homes, a meter measures and records how much gas is used, and the supplier sends out a regular bill to charge for the volume of gas used.

Liquid gas

Another way to store and transport natural gas is to first change it into a liquid. This can be done by cooling it to a temperature of about -162° centigrade. The liquefied natural gas (or LNG, as it is called) takes up 600 times less space than the gaseous form. When gas is needed, the LNG is heated so that it expands and becomes a gas again. If there is no long gas pipeline available, LNG may be an easier way of transporting natural gas, as it can be carried by ocean-going ships, for example.

At home some people have gas cookers, while others use electricity. Many people also have a gas boiler for their hot water and central heating.

The ball-shaped containers on this tanker are filled with LNG through pipelines.

USEFUL RESOURCE

Oil and natural gas are an important source of energy because they produce a great deal of heat and power when they burn. This is why petroleum is so useful as a fuel for different modes of transportation in the form of petrol, diesel oil or jet fuel.

Another major use of both oil and gas around the world is for generating electricity. In oil-fired and gas-fired power stations, oil or gas is burned to boil water and create steam. The steam turns the blades of a turbine, which drives a generator to make electricity. Together, oil and gas produce more than a quarter of the world's electrical power. The earliest power stations burned another fossil fuel – coal – and more than a third of the world's electricity is still produced using coal.

This power station in California burns natural gas to produce electricity.

Plastics

Some of the main materials made from oil and gas are plastics. All of the different kinds of plastic are made from substances called synthetic resins, which themselves come from petroleum. The resins are produced in chemical factories from oils delivered from the oil refinery. The finished plastics are usually heated, pressed, and squirted into moulds to make the final products. These range from flexible plastics used for wrapping and plastic bags, to hard substances used to make children's toys, suitcases, car interiors and many other things.

Plastics are generally light and can be squeezed into any shape, which makes them very popular with manufacturers.

Other petrochemicals

Oil and gas are also used to make all sorts of different chemicals (called petrochemicals because they are made from petroleum). These include fertilizers and pesticides that are used by farmers to increase their production of crops. Petrochemicals are also used to make a wide range of different products, such as cosmetics, detergents, dyes, inks and paints. When oil is refined, it is also used to make by-products such as wax, which can then be used for candles and polishes.

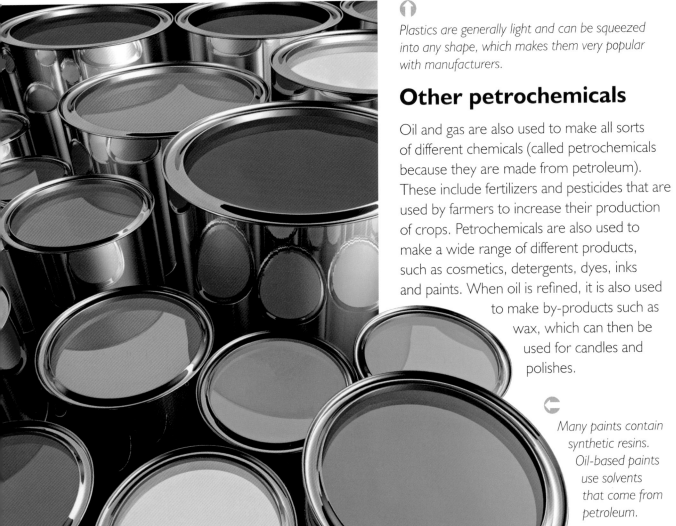

Many paints contain synthetic resins. Oil-based paints use solvents that come from petroleum.

ENVIRONMENTAL PROBLEMS

One of the main problems with fossil fuels is that they pollute the air when they are burned. Fumes from power stations and petrol engines, including the gases sulphur and nitrogen, drift high in the air. Some dissolve in the water droplets that make up clouds. This makes acid rain, which damages lakes, rivers and forests when it falls on them.

Burning fossil fuels also releases carbon dioxide, which helps to soak up and trap heat from the sun, creating a so-called 'greenhouse effect'. This has led to a gradual heating up of the world, and global warming has a great effect on the world's climate. Scientists believe that these changes are causing ice around the poles to melt, leading to a general rise in sea levels. For these reasons, environmentalists believe we should be looking at alternative sources of energy.

Steam turns back into water in these cooling towers at a British power plant. The plant's towers and chimneys release exhaust gases into the atmosphere.

Oil spills

Oil spills are disastrous for the environment. In 2001 a series of gas explosions caused the world's biggest floating oil and gas platform, called P-36, to sink off the coast of Brazil. Ten workers were killed, and oil was spilled into the ocean. In 2002, a 243-metre tanker, the *Prestige*, sank off the coast of Spain. The ship spilled a massive amount of oil and took the rest of its 77,000 tonnes to the bottom of the Atlantic Ocean. More than 900 kilometres of shoreline were affected by oil, many thousands of seabirds were killed and the coast had to be closed to fishing.

The Prestige *broke in two before sinking in 3,500 metres of water. A submarine has tried to stop more oil from leaking from the wreck.*

Caspian Sea

The Caspian Sea is the largest lake in the world, and it has been a key site for oil and gas production since the end of the 19th century, when the first offshore oil rigs were built there. Much of the oil production is off the coast of Azerbaijan, and environmentalists are concerned about pollution of the lake. Yet a new oil pipeline is being built between the Caspian and Mediterranean Seas so that oil can be more easily shipped around the world. Starting in 2005, the Baku-Tbilisi-Ceyhan (BTC) pipeline will run for 1,760 kilometres and carry a million barrels a day through Azerbaijan, Georgia and Turkey.

Oil derricks clutter and pollute the banks of the Caspian Sea.

TODAY AND TOMORROW

During the second half of the 20th century, the production of oil and natural gas increased dramatically. But today, at the beginning of the 21st century, the situation is changing. Some sources of oil and gas, such as the North Sea region, appear to be running out unless major new discoveries are made.

At the same time we are using more oil and gas every year. Experts predict that the world's known oil reserves will last for about 40 years if we keep on using oil at the same rate as today. Known natural gas reserves will last for about 60 years, with the greatest known volumes in Russia and Iran. Of course, it is possible that there are many more fossil-fuel reserves still to be discovered, but many experts do not believe this to be the case. Since there is no long-term future for fossil fuels as sources of energy, we must look for alternatives.

Almost two-thirds of the world's known oil reserves are in the Middle East, with most in Saudi Arabia.

Conserving and recycling

The world's biggest consumer of both oil and gas is the U.S., which takes up about a quarter of the world's consumption of both resources. The next-largest consumers of oil are Japan and China, and Russia and Germany consume the most natural gas. Today the world continues to rely on fossil fuels for its energy needs, but this will not always be possible. We can all help plan for the future by conserving energy and using it as efficiently as possible. A good way to help is by recycling plastics and other materials, so that we use less energy in manufacturing them.

Energy alternatives

All over the world people are already using different sources of energy. In the future cars might be able to run on fuel cells powered by hydrogen gas or engines driven by compressed air. At home we could get more electricity from solar panels, which harness the power of the sun. Many countries have developed power plants that use geothermal energy (from hot rocks beneath Earth's surface), as well as energy provided by wind, rivers, ocean waves and tides.

At this plastics recycling plant bottles and other items are sorted before being melted down and made into new products.

This home helps create some of its own electricity with solar panels on the roof.

GLOSSARY

Arctic Circle   An imaginary line that marks the boundary of the frozen region around the North Pole.

bit   A sharp tool at the end of a drill.

blow-out   A sudden rush of oil or gas from a well.

buoyancy tank   A tank full of air that helps something float on water.

by-product   Something produced as a result of producing something else.

condense   To change from a gas into a liquid.

continent   One of Earth's seven huge land masses.

crude oil   Oil as it is found naturally underground.

derrick   A framework that supports drilling equipment.

diesel   (or diesel oil) A fuel obtained from crude oil that is similar to petrol.

drill string   A series of linked steel pipes that is attached to a drill bit.

element   A substance that cannot be separated into a simpler form.

environmentalist   A person who is concerned about and acts to protect the natural environment.

extract   To take out or obtain something from a source.

fixed-leg rig   see jack-up rig.

fossil fuel   A fuel (such as oil, natural gas or coal) that comes from the remains of prehistoric plants and animals.

fractionating tower A tall column in which crude oil is separated into different substances.

fuel A substance that is burned to provide power or heat.

gas field An area where there are large reserves of natural gas that can be extracted.

gasometer A large tank used to store gas; a gasholder.

geologist A scientist who studies the structure of the Earth.

gravimeter An instrument that measures changes in the strength of Earth's gravity.

hydrocarbon A chemical compound containing hydrogen and carbon.

import To buy and bring in goods from another country.

jack-up rig An offshore oil rig with legs that can be lowered to the seabed.

liquefied natural gas (LNG) Natural gas in the form of a liquid.

magnetometer An instrument that measures changes in Earth's magnetic field.

offshore In the sea not far from the coast.

oil field An area where there are large reserves of oil that can be extracted.

petrochemical A chemical made from petroleum.

petrol A fuel used to power cars; also called gasoline or gas.

petroleum Crude oil.

plankton Tiny organisms that drift near the surface of the sea.

pocket An underground cavity where oil and/or gas are trapped.

pollution Damage caused to the environment by harmful substances.

recycle To process used material so that it can be used again.

refinery An industrial plant where oil and gas are processed and purified.

reserves Supplies that have not yet been used.

sedimentary rocks Rocks that formed from layers of sediment on the ocean floor.

seismograph An instrument that measures vibrations and shock waves.

supertanker A very large oil-carrying ship.

wildcat A test well for oil or gas.

INDEX